# Ancient Wisdom and the Measure of Our Days

## The Spiritual Dimensions of Retirement, Aging and Loss

By
Fred Brancato

Strategic Book Publishing
New York, New York

Strategic Book Publishing
An imprint of Writers Literary & Publishing Services, Inc.
845 Third Avenue, 6th Floor – 6016
New York, NY 10022
http://www.strategicbookpublishing.com

ISBN: 978-1-60693-702-0   1-60693-702-2

Printed in the United States of America

# Ancient Wisdom and the Measure of our Days

*To Leslie*

*My beloved wife and most intimate friend*

# Acknowledgements

I wish to express my thanks and appreciation to: Tom Frary, who at age ninety-four patiently listened to every word of the manuscript and offered his wise support; Mike and Wendy Laidlaw, for their editorial suggestions and insight about the receptive aspects of compassion; Betty and Ralph Smith for their encouragement to use my own voice in place of lengthy quotes from the wisdom literature; John Grace for his suggestions and encouraging communication about the book being relevant for him as a cancer survivor; Mike Brady for his affirmation about the text's relevance for the readers of his national journal; Melinda Plastas for her enthusiastic support and good counsel; Sherry Hanson for generously sharing her knowledge about the world of publishing; Patti and Paul Brassard for their friendship and ongoing creative support; Alex Clark, my father-in-law and friend who graciously reviewed the text amidst his exhausting chemotherapy; Mark Brancato, my loving son, who reviewed the publisher's contract with me; Leslie, my wife and most loving critic, who gave her considerable editorial skills to this work of the heart; and last, but not least, all the people at Strategic Book Publishing who made the publication of this book such an enjoyable experience.

*As time goes by*
*You do not care, nor I.*
*Wandering everywhere without*
*Anyone's interference*
*I feel the spring breeze*
*As I play the flute in the*
*Tavern pavilion.*

*Hu Chin Tze*
*8th Century China*

# Table of Contents

# Introduction

The title of this book is "Ancient Wisdom and the Measure of Our Days." The first part of the title, "Ancient Wisdom," refers to the vast body of recorded spiritual insight left to us by sages, mystics and saints from the world's diverse spiritual traditions. I feel profound gratitude for their lives and their generosity in sharing with us the wisdom they gained from their experiences. I am also deeply grateful to all the people, many anonymous, who over the centuries have recorded, preserved and passed-on the experiences and wisdom of these great ones. I think of them all, men and women, mystic and scribe alike, as our spiritual ancestors, and I cannot imagine what the world would be like without them and the priceless legacy they have left us.

After 50 years of ongoing study about the world views of sages, saints and mystics from diverse spiritual traditions, particularly those of the Jewish, Christian, Sufi, Taoist, Hindu, Buddhist, and Native American traditions, I continue to be delighted and inspired by how common themes always seem to emerge from their diverse voices. These common themes are the "ancient wisdom" I refer to in this presentation.

1

The second part of the title, "the measure of our days," refers to the experience of growing old. The phrase was taken from a book entitled, *The Measure of My Days* by Florida Scott-Maxwell. Florida Scott Maxwell published this book at the age of 85. Born in 1883, she lived until she was 96. *The Measure of My Days* is the most honest and insightful account about aging I have ever read. I would like to quote Florida Maxwell here in my introductory remarks, because her words set the stage for what follows.

After noting the apprehensions she and others often have about the unknown levels of deterioration of the mind and body that may come with advanced age, she wrote:

"But we also find that as we age we are more alive than seems likely, convenient, or even bearable. Too often our problem is the fervour of life within us. My dear octogenarians, how are we to carry so much life, and what are we to do with it? ....All is uncharted and uncertain, we seem to lead the way into the unknown. It can feel as though all our lives we have been caught in absurdly small personalities and circumstances and beliefs. Our accustomed shell cracks here, cracks there, and that tiresomely rigid person we supposed to be ourselves, stretches (and) expands.... Age forces us to deal with idleness, emptiness, not being needed, not able to do, helplessness just ahead perhaps.

"Here we come to a new place of which I knew nothing. We come to ... the place of release.... A long life makes me feel nearer truth, yet it won't go into words, so how can I convey it? I can't, and I want to. I want to tell people approaching and perhaps fearing age that it is a time of discovery. If they say – 'Of what?' I can only answer, 'We must each find out for ourselves, otherwise it won't be discovery.'"[1]

In finding-out for ourselves what is to be discovered in the measure of our own days, perhaps the common wisdom of sages and saints of every generation, from every corner of the world, can help.

The common themes I've chosen from our spiritual ancestors relate to what I believe are four areas of major concern to us as we age. They are: 1) change and loss in our lives; 2) our personal identity as we diminish; 3) the nature of God; and 4) how to live in the circumstances in which we find ourselves. These four areas of increasing concern as we grow older form the outline for this reflection.

Please bear in mind that the depth and scope of the subject do not allow full development of the thoughts expressed here, and while specific references will be made to only a few mystics, sages and saints, they represent what many others have said over the millennia. Also, please bear in mind that when I refer to the *diminishing* aspects of aging, I do not wish to preclude the great powers of the aging brain that are being verified these days by scientific research; which include tissue

---

1    The Measure of My Days by Florida Scott-Maxwell, Penguin Books, N.Y., 1968, pp. 138-140

regeneration, brain plasticity, more facile use of left and right sides of the brain simultaneously, and increased ability to see connections between events and circumstances (what we call wisdom).

One final preliminary note: When reflecting upon the wisdom of our spiritual ancestors, I will at times write in the first person. This is because it flows more easily and is less abstract. Also, the pronouns "I" and "my" can convey a sense of common experience among all human beings, while at the same time make room for the fact that not everyone sees or hears things in the same way.

# Chapter 1
## Change and Aging

৵

*What! Would you wish that there should be no
dried trees in the woods and no dead branches
on a tree that is growing old?*

৵

*A seventy-year-old Huron[2]*

Last January, I was fortunate enough to celebrate my 70th Birthday. Friends and acquaintances said, "You don't seem *that* old." That's nice and makes me feel good, but it makes me wonder: What is 70 (or 80 or 90) supposed to look and feel like anyway? To the young man at the deli counter who called me "Pop" the other day, I'm a pretty old guy. To Florida Maxwell at 85 or 96, I may be just a "young whipper-snapper," as Gabby Hayes would say in the old western movies. It's all so relative.

One thing I do know is that change and aging are the order of the day for people, animals and cars, to name but a few. The older I get, the more aging and change appear synonymous to

---

2   Native American Wisdom, edited by Ken Nerburn and Louise Mengelkoch, New World Library, CA, p. 56.

me. Change and aging are encoded in every cell of our bodies, and we are intimately knowledgeable about change from our every day experiences. Scientists and philosophers simply affirm what we already know: Change is the law of the universe and of the very essence of life. Our spiritual ancestors often referenced this fact as background to their testimony about the underlying presence of the Infinite, the immutable ground of all being, wherein all life and identity safely and lovingly reside.

The only difference for me between the word "change" and the word "aging" is that the word change connotes the experience of movement, with someone or something becoming different from what it was before through a transformation of some sort. Whereas aging is a mental concept often laden with the images, ideas and values of one's culture. I wonder how my own personal aging would look to me if I didn't have preconceived notions and judgments about wrinkled skin or the word, "old," and simply observed the changes going on in and around me.

Change by its very nature makes things different and therefore brings loss of some kind. As it relates to aging, change carries loss of many kinds and degrees: From loss of hair, body dexterity, and short-term memory to loss of former societal identities and opportunities available at younger ages. Unfortunately, the longer we live, the greater the odds that change will bring the dreaded and grievous loss of loved ones.

In addition to loss, change brings new opportunities and beginnings, although not always obvious at first. These opportunities, which we might even call gifts if we are fortunate to live long enough, will be examined within the context of loss often associated with aging. They come in many different forms and are unique to each person and circumstance. Whatever their outer form, these opportunities tend to offer what might be called spiritual gifts. These spiritual gifts can include such things as: a greater capacity to love and be loved, a greater ability to receive and be connected to others, and a greater sense of freedom that comes from letting go (what Florida Maxwell called "a place of release.") Most important, it seems that the ability to see and accept new opportunities and gifts that may come with loss depends in large measure upon each person's habitual view of change in everyday life.

Centuries before the birth of Jesus, Taoist monks living in the mountains of China were especially astute in pointing out that waning and waxing constitute the very fabric of change. The Western world has become somewhat familiar with the Taoist philosophical terms of Yang, the Creative, and Yin, the Receptive to describe the movement continually occurring in the universe as we know it. Within the world view of change as the interplay of Yin and Yang (polar opposites that contain one another), the Taoists of ancient China emphasized that it is Yin, the Receptive, that makes Yang, the Creative able to actualize itself. Without this earth, the sun could not grow a daisy.

I would like to share here a very personal example about the power of the receptive: When my mother, Diane, died of dementia in a nursing home, her very experienced caretaker told my wife and me, with tears in her eyes, that my mother positively affected her life more than anyone she had ever known. She said my mother had in fact changed her life. This had a powerful impact on my wife and me because my mother could do absolutely nothing for herself and barely spoke. Among all the people in a similar state whom this caregiver bathed, dressed and fed over many years, why did my mother have such a creative, life changing influence on her life? From the experience of my mother's disposition during the two years of progressive incapacitation before her death, my wife and I concluded it was the *way* my mother *completely received* everything that had to be done for her. It seems that completely receiving what someone has to give transforms both the giver and receiver, each in different ways. It's like the healing and transformative power of total, undivided listening. Being *receptive* is such a *creative* embrace of another.

Continuing with the Taoist view of change, the *I Ching* (the "Book of Changes") and the *Tao Te Ching* (the "Book of the Way") remind us that Yin is contained within Yang, and Yang within Yin. Within the ebb of an ocean's wave, flow is hidden, waiting to manifest itself. In the dead of winter, a Chan Buddhist monk can be heard saying, "Summer is here." In summer's green, snow is already on the ground. So too, when our culture's linear view of time falls from my eyes, the moment of my death is here, right now, as is the moment of my birth, and all the moments of my life, past and future. All present, right now!

The world view of past and future being present in this moment, and polar opposites containing elements of one another is also found among the traditional views of many indigenous peoples of North America, whom we collectively call Native American. It is present too in the Hindu image of Dancing Siva who, representing the power that creates and sustains the world, bears in one hand of his multiple arms a drum, and in another fire. With the vibrating drum he creates, and with fire he destroys. He is Creator and Destroyer, Destroyer and Creator. Both aspects are part of the same dance, the same transformation, the same eternal act of creation. Destruction is wedded to creation; decay leads to growth of something new. Among our spiritual ancestors, it is more than a cliché that death and birth are inseparably one. If this is true, then aging and diminishment are the process of something new being born in us and the universe.

Regarding the power of being receptive, India's Dancing Siva and China's Yin-Yang are wonderful examples of how diverse traditions can have similar views and experiences expressed in dramatically different ways. Siva represents the power that creates all in the universe. However, he, as a male figure, is completely impotent without his receptive female

consort, Sakti, who makes him capable of creating. In this regard, she is considered even more powerful than he. It is she
who makes creation possible. This view appears to be identi-
cal to the Taoist philosophy, noted a moment ago, about the
relationship of Yin and Yang. This power of the receptive is
also found in other traditions. One example, from the Christian
tradition, is Mary's "yes," her fiat, her "be it done unto me according to your word" to the movement and invitation of the
Creating Spirit to overshadow her so she could conceive, nur-
ture new life within her and give birth to someone and something great. Meister Eckhart, a 14th century scholar and mystic
cites this receptive act of Mary as a prototype of the soul and
an example of the inner transformation possible to everyone.[3]
This receptivity, this taking in, this listening and receiving is
fundamental to contemplation and prayer in the experience of
our spiritual ancestors.

This view of change has great significance for aging. If I
am receptive to the cosmic changes taking place within my
own body, and am not fooled by drying skin, shrinking muscle
mass, stiff joints, cracking bones and a host of aliments, I can
see and seize my time of old age as an opportunity for creative
growth and birth in ways I have not yet imagined.

Concerning change and aging, Buddhist tradition counsels
us to reflect on impermanence as a central fact of life. Keen

---

3    Meister Eckhart, translated by Raymond Blakney, 1941, Harper and Row,
N.Y.

awareness of change and impermanence seems to have sparked the transformative experience of Siddhartha Gotama, the Buddha, when he sat under a tree in India's pre-dawn light, six centuries before the birth of Jesus. Tradition tells us that in a flash (as so often happens in mystical experiences) time disappeared into eternity and Siddhartha knew with certainty the root cause of suffering and grief so common to the human condition. He later told his followers, in so many words, that suffering comes from living in denial of change and clutching and clinging to what is passing.

Thinking and behaving as though stability and well being are found on the surface of what I see, touch and feel is the great illusion referenced not only by Siddhartha, but by the nameless sages, or "seers," of his Hindu tradition. This is also a centuries old realization among mystics of diverse spiritual traditions. They too felt everything, absolutely everything in the world of appearances is passing and this fact of life should become an integral part of a person's world view and way of living. Mistaking the temporal for the eternal, and thereby clinging to it, is delusional and *the* source of suffering.

Lao Tzu (reputed author of the 6th Century B.C. Chinese classic, *Tao Te Ching*) left us these simple words, which capture the message of many sages and saints throughout the ages: "If you realize that all things change, there is nothing you will try to hold on to."[4] It seems that the flow of change in my body

---

4    Tao Te Ching by Lao Tzu, Translated by Stephen Mitchell, Harper Perennial,

and mind, called aging, naturally nudges, maybe even enables, me to follow the good counsel of this Taoist sage. In a similar vein, I'm further advised by an anonymous Hindu sage of the Upanishads not to grieve over what is unavoidable.

In Hindu tradition, there are four stages in a full life. Each one marks major transitions through identifiable stages of social, psychological and spiritual growth. The first stage is that of "the student," whose work is to learn how to become a member of society. The second stage is that of the "householder." This is the stage of involvement in the day-to-day responsibilities of employment, raising a family and pursuing a career. The third stage is that of the "forest dweller." It is the stage when one leaves the preoccupations of the "householder" and turns to what is beyond the mainstream dance of daily living. In this stage a person may find him or herself entering a physical, psychological and spiritual forest hitherto unknown. In our terms, this is the time of retirement and beyond.

Successful completion of the forest dweller stage (a spiritual stage as well as a situational one), leads to the fourth stage, the hardest to attain and the one that few people ever reach, short of death itself. It is the stage or the state of the "samnyasin." The samnyasin is a person who totally lets go and leaves all things behind, becoming virtually naked in every way, stripped of all physical possessions, thoughts, judgments, and even one's ego self.

---

N.Y., #74.

As far as I can tell, the internal state of the Hindu samnya-sin is similar to the ideal spiritual state described in different terms by Buddhists, Taoists, Sufis (from the mystical tradition of Islam), Kabbalists (from the mystical tradition of Judaism) and Christians as "emptiness," "no self," "annihilation of the self," and the two Gospel phrases "he who looses his life will find it" and "it is no longer I who live…"

The forest dweller and the samnyasin stages of life are especially relevant for the experience of aging. Retirement and aging into advanced years appear to mirror the spiritual journey described by mystics of all traditions because they tend to strip a human being down and away from the everyday world and self identities that once adorned the younger person. This stripping away of familiar things, circumstances and identities *is* the forest one enters, and it is the realm of the spiritual wanderer where there are trails personally not tread before and few landmarks to help find the way. I recall here the words of Florida Maxwell, quoted earlier, about old age: "All is uncharted and uncertain, we seem to lead the way into the unknown."

In this sense, the unstoppable current of aging can be seen as aiding the spiritual work of my own resisting will. Again, in Florida Maxwell's words, "Age forces us to deal with idleness, emptiness, (and) not being needed…" While doing things to keep me healthy and vital both physically and mentally, perhaps I'm called on a deeper level by my retirement and advancing age to accept diminishment (however slow or fast) and

13

embrace it as an opportunity to follow the advice of my spiritual ancestors. In harmony with their advice, perhaps I should see all the changes and emerging circumstances I didn't plan for within a much bigger context and as an opportunity for freedom of a kind I have never known.

# Chapter 2
## Aging and Human Identity

*The petal of a blossom never comes forth alone,*
*but unimpededly takes in all related parts of the*
*blooming tree. This petal must dissolve itself,*
*thus entering into all and taking in all.*

*Fa tsang, 7ᵗʰ Century China[5]*

The challenges of advanced aging are truly formidable, as people often find themselves in circumstances they neither imagined, nor were fully prepared to live in. While the experience of never being fully prepared for what life brings is common to every stage of life, it seems most profoundly true for living into old age.

Rising in the morning to a life in retirement is significantly different from waking to a day on the job. While it can be experienced at any age, the experience of my own personal mortality in retirement and advancing age is significantly

---

5    Creativity and Taoism, A Study of Chinese Philosophy, Art, and Poetry by Chang Chung-yuan, Harper Torchbooks, 1970, p. 12.

different in character from previous times in my life. It can take the form of waking up to what might be called my naked existence, unclothed by the usual identities created over a lifetime. The ideas and conventions of thought that have feathered my nest and made me safe from the awesomeness and terror of my existence, an existence I did not create, seem to erode and fall away with time. Evelyn Underhill, in her classic study on mysticism, says it well: "Consciousness shrinks in terror from contact with the mighty verb 'to be.'"[6]

In my retirement and old age, there are fewer and fewer places for me to hide from my incomprehensible existence and the passing it entails of what I have known as me and my life. While this nakedness can be frightening, if not terrifying, it can also be, at the same time, freeing and vitalizing.

This experience of my existence, unclothed by acculturated meanings and social identities, also brings profound sadness. This kind of existential sadness that an older person may feel is described by the anonymous author of the spiritual classic, *The Cloud of Unknowing*. Writing in 14th Century England from within the Christian tradition, he notes that "deep, interior sorrow" is the most appropriate response to this "naked knowing feeling" of "one's own being." He wrote, "Every man has plenty of cause for sorrow but he alone understands the deep universal reason for sorrow who experiences *that he is*.... He alone feels authentic sorrow who realizes not only *what he is*

---

6    Mysticism by Evelyn Underhill, Image Books Doubleday, N.Y., 1990, p. 9.

but *that he is.*" He then went on to write, "Anyone who has not felt this should really weep, for he has never experienced real sorrow." Lest we think this was written by a depressed person, the reason he gives for weeping at the absence of this "real sorrow" is that it "purifies" and "prepares" the heart for the joy that comes from transcending oneself.[7]

Transcending oneself, losing one's life in order to find it, dying in order to live, letting go of everything, including my life as I've known it, involves, in Sufi terms, the "annihilation" of my separate, ego-self that I'm so attached to. Letting go of my separate ego self is experienced by sages and saints as the *only* path to realization of my true nature and identity as a human being. From this larger point of view, the involuntary stripping down experiences of aging, with the fear and profound sorrow they engender, offer opportunities for freedom from my constricted, limited self and for communion with the All, the Absolute, the Great Mystery of which our ancestors spoke.

All spiritual traditions in one form or another emphasize this stripping away of the layers of oneself as a prerequisite for enlightenment and the experience of communion with the all pervading Godhead, however we define Him, Her, or It. Mystics from the Buddhist, Christian, Sufi, and Kabbalistic traditions are perhaps the most articulate on this point. However, I

---

7   The Cloud of Unknowing, edited by William Johnson, Image Books, Doubleday, N.Y., p. 103.

think no one expressed this more emphatically than the Sufi, Shaykh ad-Darqawi, who dramatically challenged the illusory belief that we have our own existence. After getting my attention by saying I'm a "mirage" in the desert and "extinct" before I'm "extinguished," he emphatically stated that being in itself is God's not mine. He said I'm like an onion. If I peel away all the layers there would be nothing left of the onion. So too if I peeled away all the layers I think are my own separate self there would be nothing left but God.[8]

If a person gives-up attachment to a separate ego-self and assumes the vantage point expressed by Shaykh ad-Darqawi, the natural forces of aging and deterioration can be seen as part of the emanation and re-absorption, ebb and flow, of the Self-Existent ("Self-Existent" is one of the several Hindu terms for God). Many traditions describe the Self- Existent as Love Itself. According to the wisdom of our ancestors, if this becomes my way of seeing and *experiencing* the world and what I take to be myself and God, it can actually bring peace and joy and a sense of Infinite Love's embrace of me and all that I am.

Many ancestors have testified to the spiritual nature of diminishment and disintegration of oneself. One such person was Pierre Teilhard de Chardin, a scientist, priest and mystic who lived in our lifetime. In a prayerful passage from his book, *The Divine Milieu*, he wrote this about his own aging: "When

---

8    Letters of a Sufi Master, The Shaykh ad-Darqawi, Translated by Titus Burckhardt, Fons Vitae, 1998.

the signs of age begin to mark my body (and still more when they touch my mind); when the ill that is to diminish me or carry me off strikes from without or is born within me; when the painful moment comes in which I suddenly awaken to the fact that I am growing ill or old; and above all at that last moment when I feel I am losing hold of myself and am absolutely passive within the great unknown forces that have formed me; in all those dark moments, O God, grant that I may understand that it is you who are painfully parting the fibers of my being in order to penetrate to the very marrow of my substance and bear me away within Yourself."[9]

This paring-down or stripping away of what we thought to be ourselves is directly related to realizing our true nature, or "original face," in Taoist and Chan Buddhist terminology. Personal experience of mental and physical decline in me or those I know, make me ask: Am I my ability to think? Am I my thoughts, my mind, my ability to function? Am I my social abilities, my ability to speak and walk and take care of myself? Am I my looks, my eyes, my legs, my hands, my teeth, my skin? Am I someone's spouse, parent, sibling, or child? Who am I *really*? And, who or what is God *anyway*? In the forest in which I now find myself, the answers that once sustained me are not working the way they did in my "student" and "house-holder" days.

---

9  The Divine Milieu by Pierre Teilhard De Chardin, Harper and Row, N.Y.p.62.

Regarding these questions about identity and the nature of ultimate reality, the first thought that comes to mind is: *Where do I look?* Our spiritual ancestors answer in one collective and authoritative voice: "Look *inside* yourself!" they say. Beyond the process of psycho-therapy what does this looking inside myself really mean, especially since Zen masters enjoy reminding us that there really is no "inside" or "outside." Be that as it may, looking inside has risks. I may find, as many mystics have, a pitch dark night and an unnerving silence that does not offer recognizable answers and images found more readily in what I take to be outside me among the people, circumstances, things and ideas that make-up my familiar world.

Further, I am dimly aware that this very deep look inside may have consequences that radically change me and how I see the world I'm so attached to. It may be one thing for Zen masters to encourage, but another thing to do. This is a scary prospect for it requires letting go of my ego self and my preconceived notions. Do I really want that? My fear makes me say, "Not really."

Powerful images of fear block my way to letting go. Regarding fear, Hindu sacred scriptures are clear in saying, as do other written traditions, that fear disappears when I truly experience myself as one with the All, and I no longer see myself as separate from the rest of creation. In the following quote from the Upanishads, the "Self" means the presence of God or Brahman at the core of each of us: "When a man finds his existence and unity in the Self ...who is the basis of life...who is inexpressible beyond all predicates, then alone does he transcend all fear."[10]

Hindu sages may sing about the glories of experiencing God at the core of me and letting go of fear, but absent this experience of my underlying identity, I often feel powerless to get free of the fear that dangles me in its jaws. Feeling powerlessness in the face of my fears, there is, in nearly all traditions, explicit recognition of human frailty, and, with few exceptions, the need for divine help. The word for divine assistance that is most familiar to us in the Western world is grace.

Definitions of grace generally have three elements: First, it involves unconditional help from a higher power that is not contingent upon merit; second, it involves a free, un-coerced and open response from the person receiving it; and third, it is an expression of the Godhead's unconditional love. In other words, grace is essentially a *relationship* with the Infinite, and, according to mystics of every generation, that infinite source of all being resides at the center of me. Thus, the place to look for help is within.

This notion of grace that "saves a wretch like me" (as the song says) also finds beautiful expression in the figure of Amitaba Buddha (the "Buddha of Infinite Light") found in Japan's Shin Buddhism. There is the saying, "Namu Amida Butsu,"

---

10   The Upanishads, translated by Swami Prabhavananda and Frederick Manchester, Signet Classic, 2002, p. 56.

which means, "I entrust my weak, limited self to the Buddha of Infinite Light." Most relevant to my point here about identity and looking inward, is the insight of the great scholar and Zen master, D.T. Suzuki, who was raised in the Shin tradition. In a letter to a friend he asserts that the Buddha of Infinite Light resides *within* each of us and, in a way that is beyond our comprehension, *is* each of us.[11]

I see strong parallels between Amitaba Buddha, the Cosmic Christ of Christianity, and the Atman of Hinduism. In Hinduism, Brahman (the Godhead and source of all creation) resides in "the lotus of my heart." My true self is the Self of Brahman, and Atman is the Sanskrit term that points to this experience. Thus, in a paradoxical way, when it comes to needing divine assistance in my human frailty, sages and saints once again point to the very depths within me that are so frightening and need divine assistance to explore. And so, the grace to transcend the fear of death and my naked existence confronting me in a special way in my retirement and old age is found in the realization of my self as a manifestation of the Infinite, especially the Infinite experienced as Love Itself. Herein lies my "original face."

Advanced aging and living in greater proximity to death can be seen as a gift of grace that helps me let go and look to something greater than the tiny and nebulous experience I call

---

11 Buddha of Infinite Light by D.T. Suzuki, Shambala Publications, London, 1997. p. 38.

myself. I'm reminded again of Florida Maxwell's words about aging quoted earlier, "It can feel as though all our lives we have been caught in absurdly small personalities and circumstances and beliefs. Our accustomed shell cracks here, cracks there, and that tiresomely rigid person we supposed ourselves to be, stretches (and) expands…"

In pursuing a little further the advice of our spiritual ancestors to look inside for our true identity, I would like to cite an experience of Pierre Teilhard de Chardin, which has stayed with me ever since I read it 46 years ago. He described his experience as taking a lamp and descending deep down into himself where the everyday occupations, relationships and identities familiar to him faded away. When he could go no further because the steps faded from beneath his feet, he came to what he called a "bottomless abyss" from whence the source of his life came. (It's interesting to note that although he was a Jesuit priest, he never used the name God. I sense this is because he entered a realm where names and concepts were too small and couldn't convey what he experienced.) He then returned to the light of day and the familiar, comfortable surroundings of his life. However, to his surprise, he found that the Ineffable Mystery he experienced at the core of him was present too in what he called the "innumerable strands" that formed the "very stuff" of his daily life. In his words, "it was the same mystery, I recognized it without a doubt." To him, these were the same strands that were also changing him, aging him, transforming him, bringing him home.[12]

The key element in Chardin's experience — discovery of the Infinite at the core of him and all things in the universe — is similar to the discovery of many mystics over the millennia: Everything in the universe is a manifestation of the Absolute, the Self-Existent or however else we name it. Nothing would be were it not a manifestation of the Infinite. The meaning of the Muslim expression, "There is no God but Allah," according to the 14th century Sufi mystic and scholar, Ibn Arabi, is that nothing exists but Allah. If Allah (one of the many Muslim names for God) removed His, Her, Its presence from anything, it would cease to be.[13] To paraphrase the words of Shaihk Ad Darqawi, what ever gave us the idea we had our own separate existence in the first place? The revered Christian scholar and saint, Thomas Aquinas, said the same thing in language of the scholastic philosophy of his time. And Rabia of Basra, a 13th century Sufi saint and poet put it most beautifully, "How do I say this: God and I will forever cherish Myself."[14] (Myself is spelled with a capital M.) She realized that she had no existence apart from God.

---

12    The Divine Milieu, De Chardin, pp. 48,49.

13    Alone With the Alone, Creative Imagination in the Sufism of Ibn Arabi by Henry Corbin, Princeton University Press, Princeton, N.J., 1969.

14    Love Poems from God, translated by Daniel Ladinsky, Penguin Compass, N.Y., 2002, p. 18.

The view of sages and saints that God is the only existence and that our lives are essentially manifestations of the Infinite Itself is related to the world view of eternal return pervading many spiritual traditions. This has great significance for how I see change and aging. In a way, returning to the source begins at birth. It is the innate destiny of all manifestations or emanations of the Divine to return from whence they came. It's like sparks bursting from a bonfire and returning to their source, to use a Hindu analogy; or to use the analogy of a Zen master, it's like a river going over a thousand foot waterfall: the water separates into parts as it descends, while remaining water, and becomes the river again when it reaches the bottom. As Moses Cordovero, a Jewish Kabballist of 16th century Spain noted, "Each day of your life is adorned with supernal return."[15]

Continuing with the theme of eternal return and its relevance for aging and identity, the Taoists speak of all things as emanating from the Grand Void (Wu Chi), also called the One, the Unmanifest beyond which nothing exists. The Grand Void manifests itself in Tai Chi, the Grand Ultimate, which, in Taoist terms, is the world of "10,000 things." In an endless ebb and flow rhythm, all that is manifest in Tai Chi returns to Wu Chi. Lao Tzu, in 500 B.C. linked this eternal return to how we ought to live when he wrote in the *Tao Te Ching*, "Each separate being in the universe returns to the common source. Returning

---

15    The Essential Kabbalah, compiled and translated by Daniel C. Matt, Castle Books, 1997, p. 87.

to the source is serenity. If you realize where you come from... you can deal with whatever life brings you, and when death comes, you are ready."[16]

Catherine of Genoa, the 15th century Christian saint and mystic, described her experience of serenity upon return to the source in the following way: "the state of the soul is ... of such utter peace and tranquility that it seems to her that her heart, and her bodily being, and all both within and without are immersed in an ocean of utmost peace..."[17] Catherine indicated that her experience of ineffable peace was the result of having been "naught," her term for the "emptiness" and "self extinction" described by Zen masters and Sufi saints.

While very far from the state of "emptiness," or being "naught," I do know from my own experience, that when I let go of myself and accept whatever is given, without striving to be other than what and where I am in life at that moment, I feel a great sense of peace and serenity. Self surrender leading to serenity is a much better way than the rigidness so conducive to resentment and bitterness.

Regarding this universal theme among our spiritual ancestors that we emanate from, are sustained by and return to the unmanifest source of all being, there are two related, bottom line implications for aging: The first is related to identity

---

16    Tao Te Ching, Stephen Mitchell translation, #16.

17    Mysticism by Evelyn Underhill, Image Books, Doubleday, N.Y., 1990, p. 441.

because identity derives from where we originate, where we are destined to return and wherein our very existence resides. My true identity is found in being a manifestation of the Infinite. This is especially relevant to aging as the social identities of my student and householder days are stripped away in my life as a forest dweller.

The second implication here for aging is that the One, the All, the Infinite, however it is named, is imminent, present, manifest in all beings, things and circumstances in every moment and, therefore, is present and manifest in all the changes associated with aging. In this regard, I'd like to recall Chardin's experience and belief that it was the Godhead at the very core of him who was parting the fibers of his being in his aging process and bringing him back from whence he came. Having been exhaled, so to speak, by the divine, he was now being inhaled; having flowed forth, he was now ebbing back into the sea, and that sea (which I cannot note often enough) is defined by sages and saints as Infinite Love.

As I face all the changes in identity stimulated by the circumstances of aging, I recall that my spiritual ancestors say, in no uncertain terms, I am eternal. At the core of me, at the infinite center, is the Absolute. They tell me that my identity, my true nature, derives from the very source of being itself, however we name it.

I see another implication here that has relevance for the loneliness sometimes felt in advanced age. It is related to the loss of loved ones and all who have gone before us, as well as those we will leave behind when we pass-on. If I accept the world view that the All, the Unmanifest, the Godhead, in Whom everyone and everything exists eternally, is at the center of me -- is the very *substance* of me -- then within me too is all that is, has ever been or ever will be, including all who have gone before me and all who will come after me. I'm eternally bound to them as I am to the Infinite. They may feel distant, but existentially they are not; though unmanifest, they are (to use a phrase from the Quran pertaining to Allah) as close as the vein in my neck. I am as connected to them as I have always been. The sense I get from reading the collective works of our spiritual ancestors, and sometimes from my own experience, is that there is a very thin veil between time and eternity.

Were I to assume the world view of my spiritual ancestors, my identity, would, in large measure, reside in my connection to the cosmos. When Zen Buddhists practice shikantaza (a form of meditation called "just sitting") they remind themselves of the Taoist insight that what is in the macrocosm is in the microcosm and what is in the microcosm is in the macrocosm. Hindu sages have explicitly said this as did mystics from other traditions. Because I have no being apart from the One, the All, wherever I sit, I reside at the heart of the universe. It's all there because the Infinite One is there. This center is everywhere and nowhere. I especially love the way the Navajo describe a person whose consciousness resides at the center and who *lives* in harmony with all that is there: Such a person is said to be Honzo, "Walking in Beauty."[18]

When talking about human identity, the philosophical terms often used in place of the word, "God," such as the Infinite, the All, the Absolute, the God-head, the Self-Existent, and the like, can feel cold, distant and impersonal. It can be hard to find a sense of intimacy and identity in them. However, there were many devotional names used by our spiritual ancestors that better captured the intimacy they experienced with the Godhead, and that express an identity that comes from this relationship. They include such names as Tunkasila (Lakota for Grandfather) or Oya Sama (Japanese for Dearest Mother/ Father or Dearest Parent), "Friend" in the Sufi tradition, and "Beloved" in the Jewish and Christian traditions.

All I've said thus far about our ancestor's view of themselves as manifestations of the Infinite implies a personal identity that is constitutionally deeper than that of being a "child" of God. My notion of a child involves a life not contingent upon the life of the parent, an independent way of living and a social and psychological identity that he or she has and grows into. What the sages and mystics of diverse spiritual traditions say about our relationship to the infinite seems to go deeper. They say we are *manifestations,* expressions of God in a way that is existentially dependent, eternal, and utterly beyond our

---

18    The American Indian Mind in a Linear World by Donald Fixico, Routledge, N.Y., 2003, pp. 63-73.

comprehension. The emptiness of one's ego-self that leads to this realization can move a person to the seemingly blasphemous experience that his or her existence and the Existence which *is* the Godhead Itself are inseparably one. It is an intimacy of such depth that it is hard even to imagine, let alone comprehend. Yet it was experienced by mystics and saints of every tradition. The point I wish to make here is this: *Because I have this kind of innate intimacy with the Infinite, there is nothing that can detract or add to what I am.* It is this kind of intimacy, this kind of identity, that I want to remember when I'm feeling useless, not needed or on the shelf in retirement and old age.

Among Hindus, the statements attributed to Jesus in the Gospels, that he and God (his "Abba Father," Abba being an expression of intimacy) are one and the same express the highest form of conscious about the true nature and identity of every human being. It is realization of one's identity as the Atman, or "Brahman within."

Meister Eckhart seems to have experienced this kind of consciousness and identity when he boldly stated: "I am that I was and that I shall remain now and forever....for in this breakthrough I find that God and I are both the same.... If anyone does not ...find this truth in himself he cannot understand what I have said – for it is a discovered truth which comes immediately from the heart of God."[19]

---

19    Meister Eckhart, translated by Raymond B. Blakney, Harper Perennial, N.Y., 1941, pp 231, 232.

Based upon their *experiences* and not their abstract thoughts, this is what many of our spiritual ancestors say in differing ways is my original face, my true nature, my Buddha nature, and wherein my life and identity rests. If I trust their experiences and what they say about them, this then is the reality and personal identity hidden beneath my aging body and brain that are melting back into the cosmos and "returning" to the Self-Existent. I remember here the refrain of the *Upanishads*: "The Self-Existent is the source of all felicity. Who could live, who could breathe, if that blissful Self dwelt not within the lotus of the heart? He it is that gives joy."[20]

---

20   The Upanishads, translated by Swami Probhavananda and Frederick Manchester, Signet Classic, 2002, p. 56, VII, Taittiriya

# Chapter 3
## The Nature of the Great Mystery

∂

*If the doors of perception were cleansed,*
*everything would appear as it is, infinite.*

∾

*William Blake,*
*18ᵗʰ century English poet*

Our spiritual ancestors clearly understood that no intelligence of any kind could possibly understand the nature of God. It would be like trying to fit all the oceans of the world into a tiny hole dug in the sand. The Self-Existent, the unmanifest source of all life is hidden in unbreakable silence and darkness that no light of intelligence can penetrate, as Jan Ruysbroeck, the 14ᵗʰ century Christian mystic noted. Were it not so, the Absolute, the Great Mystery would not be "that which is," and we would not be creatures.

The Tao Te Ching's first words are, "The Tao that can be told is not the Eternal Tao," and the approach to the unknown of Buddhism's great masters is found in their often repeated phrase, "not this, not that." This Buddhist phrase, in turn, sounds similar to the "I am who am" response given to Moses when he sought to understand the infinite reality he experienced in a common bush.

Conceptual understanding of its very nature is limited and the sages and saints of nearly every persuasion encourage us to give up philosophical knowing. Does this mean then that my hunger for the Ineffable is doomed to be unrequited? Quite the contrary! What is so encouraging about this ancestral advice that we cannot possibly *know* or understand the Great Mystery with our minds, is the even stronger affirmation that we can *experience* it. In the words of a Buddhist sage, "We can't know it, but we can be it." And it is precisely this "not knowing" (a Taoist phrase) that enables me to be it. Lao Tzu writes in the Tao Te Ching, "In the pursuit of knowledge, everyday something is added. In the practice of Tao, everyday something is dropped."[21]

The *experience* of communion with the Great Mystery within me, and everyone and everything in the universe is far superior to knowing some isolated, abstract concepts that are not the things thought to be known. Further, ideas and concepts by their nature keep the objects of my limited mind separate from me. As we have seen, our ancestors report from their experiences that we are constitutionally one with and inseparable from the infinite source of everything. We just need to wake up

---

21    Tao Te Ching, Stephen Mitchell translation, #48.

to what is already present. This is what it means to be a "Buddha," an "awakened one."

Emphasis among our spiritual ancestors on experience and not the abstract thoughts of philosophy is exemplified by Siddhartha Gotama, the Buddha. His focus was on how to live here and now in this moment. This man, who by all accounts had an astonishing mind, concluded that the pursuit of consciousness through philosophical speculation was in fact a distraction and an abstraction which could not lead to freedom and realization of the Reality underlying this world of change. Enlightenment in his experience was not intellectual understanding. The nature of ultimate reality was not a mystery to figure out, nor a problem to solve. Rather, realization of one's true nature and the embracing presence of the Infinite were *experiential* and *relational*. In the momentary states of emptiness experienced by our spiritual ancestors, thoughts or concepts vanished. All the "what's, why's and wherefore's" were no more. This state of emptiness allowed the experience of being one with the All. In this experience of oneness with the eternal the ego-self melts into infinite love and infinite wisdom.

*The thing about this is that there is no puzzle,*
*no problem, and really no 'mystery'....all*
*matter, all life, is charged with dharmakaya...*

*everything is emptiness, everything is*
*compassion. I don't know when in my life I've*
*ever had such a sense of beauty.*

*Thomas Merton, a Christian monk describing*
*an experience he had in Sri Lanka[22]*

Love and wisdom are the supreme human *states of being* in other traditions as well. While the experience of love and wisdom are critical for life and identity at every age, I think they are especially relevant for aging because in old age one can feel lonely and out of the mainstream, with the idleness, emptiness and feeling of not being needed that Florida Maxwell referred to in our opening quotes of her. Love and wisdom are especially relevant because they are the experience of connection and being part of something much bigger than oneself. Wisdom is *consciousness* of the oneness and inter-being of all things. Love is the *state of oneness* with all things. In my heart of hearts love makes wisdom possible and each, if not the same thing, is in the other. Both wisdom and love find their expression in compassion.

---

22    Thoughts on the East by Thomas Merton, New Directions, N.Y., 1965, pp. 83, 84. "Dharmakaya" is a Sanskrit term of Mahayana Buddhism referencing the unmanifest or unseen source of all creation, which can be experienced as infinite love, compassion and wisdom beyond all thought.

Exploring this a little further, the human experience of love as *agape* (the Greek word for love in the Christian tradition), or *karuna* (the Sanskrit term for the compassion that holds all things in creation), or *Tz'u* (the Chinese word for the love or "great sympathy" that creates and sustains the universe) is the kind of love that I'm referring to. Experience of this love is calm and still, infinitely open and infinitely inclusive. There are no dichotomies, because it embraces all things as one. When I experience love, I'm experiencing in a finite way the manifestation and presence of God. This is what makes love a state of oneness with all things. I see compassion as the creative human acts of giving and receiving that flow from consciousness of this oneness, this love. In their own way, expressions of kindness are akin to compassion in that they too are expressions of the all embracing oneness of being.

The inextricably connected human qualities of love, compassion and wisdom dimly reflect the nature of the Infinite. Since the Self-Existent *is* all that is, it does not *have* love or wisdom, because *having* something implies that it is separate from oneself. The Absolute, the Self-Existent is what it is, therefore It has nothing; It *is* everything; it is the "I am who am" of Moses. It is the experience of many mystics, and not just their philosophical speculation, that God *is* Infinite Love and *is* Infinite Wisdom. Further, it is their experience, as already noted, that love and wisdom are one and the same without distinction.

However, even to use these terms — to predicate anything of the Self-Existent — is not to capture the reality. These terms are, as Buddhists would say, only "fingers pointing to the moon," but they are *not* the moon. Nevertheless, the Infinite Reality beyond the term "love" — and forever beyond the comprehension of any created entity — can be experienced when all that one knows drops away and there is the conceptless experience of eternity, or in Hindu terminology, Nirvana.

# Chapter 4
## Ways of Living

☙

*Then a Voice said,*
*'Behold this day, for it is yours to make'*

❧

*Black Elk, Lakota (1863-1950)*[23]

The common experiences and world views of our spiritual ancestors regarding the nature of change, human identity and God, informed the ways of living they espoused. Among these, there are three in particular that I think have special relevance for aging. They are: 1) detachment, 2) being in the present moment, and 3) love (which encompasses wisdom and compassion). All three are connected, and if there is one word or way that captures the other two, it is love.

First, detachment: Detachment is a word that pervades the writings of our spiritual ancestors. As I understand it, it is a state of being that our ancestors saw as central to wisdom and love. Detachment is not indifference. Quite the contrary, it is

---

23    Black Elk Speaks, by Nicholas Black Elk, as recorded and translated by John G. Neihardt, University of Nebraska Press 1979, Lincoln and London p. 33.

the basis for connection and communion. Detachment, in so many words, is the letting go of one's isolated ego-self which involves the cessation of clutching or clinging to things and circumstances. If I flip the word "detachment" over, like a coin, the words on the other side are freedom and compassion.

Detachment is found in Siddhartha's third noble truth, letting go of desire in order to free oneself from suffering in this world of change. Lao Tzu observed, as we noted earlier, that there is nothing to hold onto since all is changing. For him, the person of Tao lets all things come and lets all things go. Detachment is Francis of Assisi's "lady poverty," the same poverty Meister Eckhart describes as emptiness of self when he spoke about the Gospel beatitude, "blessed are the poor in spirit." Detachment is found on the Buddhist, Sufi, and Kabbalist paths to the state of emptiness and self annihilation, wherein a person's ego-self, pre-conceived ideas and judgments are transcended. It is found, too, in the generosity, selfless service and communion of the Lakota with all their ancestors — and the ancestors of which they spoke are every created entity of Wakan Tanka, the Great Spirit.

This kind of detachment seems especially relevant for aging because it involves letting go of my separate ego-self with all the former identities and capacities that are naturally dissipating in my retirement and metamorphosis into old age. It frees me up to receive the spiritual gifts that are given in the midst of loss. This kind of detachment helps me transcend my tiny, isolated self and allows me to experience freedom and peace as part of an infinitely larger process that is embracing me.

The second way of living especially relevant to aging is being in the present moment. All the aspects of detachment just referenced, seem to enable living in the present moment. When truly detached, I'm not clinging to the past or worried about the future. Because I've let go of myself and feel an integral part of what is larger than me, fear no longer inhibits me from being present to what is before me. I'm freer to receive, appreciate, marvel at, and enjoy the everyday, commonplace circumstances that come my way in each moment, because I'm not held prisoner by my pre-conceived notions and judgments. I'm free too from bitterness and regret that things are different from what I wanted. To live fully in the moment is its own reward, made possible by detachment from my separate, ego-self.

The third and consummate way of living relevant to people of all ages, but especially for those living into retirement and advanced age, is love, as described above. Love (encompassing wisdom and compassion) unlocks the experience of isolation and connects a person to everything. This experience of connection does not require the presence of other people. It is a state of being! A monk living as a hermit can experience profound connection to every one and every thing. Detachment or freedom from my tiny self leads to the experience of affinity, interconnectedness and oneness with all things within the Great Sympathy. Love involves inter-being with "all my relations." Following the orientation of America's indigenous peoples, this includes both my Aunt Mary and the little ants with multiple legs that walk along the ground and want to share my picnic sandwich. All that has been said about love and compassion as veiled expressions of the Infinite leads me to the conclusion that I am most myself when I love.

The acts of compassion that flow from love have two inseparable dimensions: giving and receiving. Giving and receiving both reflect the nature of inter-being and the oneness of things.... and each is contained within the other, as yin and yang are. In this regard, a dear friend recently shared with me his insight about compassion and aging that deeply touched me. He saw receiving as an act of compassion and observed that as we advance in age, our acts of compassion naturally assume the receiving dimension, as they did with my mother. If you will recall, I referenced her story earlier when speaking about the creative power of the receptive. My mother's compassionate act of receiving matched her caretaker's compassionate act of giving, and there occurred between them a profoundly creative, life-giving connection, like soil receiving a seed. Receiving is active not passive. It takes in and enfolds what is given. This kind of compassion — this expression of love — is especially relevant for how to live into advanced age.

As this book ends, I would like to reference our spiritual ancestors' emphasis on the profound spiritual significance of day-to-day menial tasks. There is a Zen saying that I especially love: "In chopping wood and carrying water, therein lies the beautiful Tao." In the common daily actions and rituals of living, such as cooking, eating, getting dressed, paying bills and bathing, therein lies the Eternal, the Great Sympathy, the Friend. And if I advance to where I cannot do these things for myself — and maybe don't know who my caretakers are, or even that I'm being cared for — there too is the Ineffable, the Great Mystery, Wakan Tanka. Even in these circumstances, I am that which I have always been. I'm in the process of returning to the Unmanifest, being re-absorbed by the embrace of the Infinite, the Great Sympathy. This is the collective wisdom of sages and saints.

The closing words of this reflection about living fully the measure of our days, come from Yunus Emre, a 13th century Sufi poet who lived in Turkey.[24] I've collected just a few lines from his many poems and put them together like flowers in a bouquet. They contain much of what has been said, and I invite you to sit back and take them in during the pause between each. They are offered here as follows:

෪

*Only the word 'I' divides me from God*

෫

---

24    The Drop That Became The Sea, Lyric Poems of Yunis Emre, translated by Kabir Helminski and Refik Agan, Threshold books, Vermont, 1989.

*Oh Friend, when I began to love you*
*my intellect went and left me.*

*A soul in love is free of worries.*

*Let's love and be loved.*
*No one inherits the world.*

*I am the drop that contains the ocean.*

*No longer do I mourn*
*or cloud my heart,*
*because truth's voice is heard*
*and I'm at my own wedding.*

To whom or what am I being wed in my advancing age? Recalling Florida Maxwell: "We must each find out for ourselves, otherwise it won't be discovery."

# Follow-up Questions

The following questions are offered as a vehicle for further reflection and group discussion. They may also facilitate a second reading of this compact book.

1. What do you fear most about growing old? Was there anything in the book that allayed your fears or comforted you?

2. What are the stereotypical images of aging in our culture? How do they affect the way you see yourself and others?

3. Is it possible to move beyond the notions of aging in our culture and beyond the physical-mental realities of advanced age to embrace them as part of a process bigger than we are? If so, what would be the benefits? What would it take to do so?

4. How does our culture teach us to manage loss? How do you manage loss emotionally and spiritually? What does it help to think about, remember and do when managing loss of any kind?

5.  As you grow older, do you find it easier or more difficult to "let go"? Why?

6.  Ancient wisdom notes the power of "the Receptive" and the ability to receive as central to creativity and compassion. Have you had experiences that support this?

7.  In your experience of caring for someone who was ill or infirm, what did you find most difficult? What did you find most meaningful?

8.  When someone took care of you, what did you find most difficult? What did you find most meaningful?

9.  How can a person accept changes in old age as an opportunity to receive when our society surrounds us with messages to be independent and not be a burden? What does the message of being a "burden" imply?

10. What do you feel gives you worth? Has this changed with aging? Why?

11. Can you think of examples that link diminishment and death to growth and development of something new?

12. Have you ever pared-down your possessions either voluntarily or involuntarily? How has that experience affected you?

13. The book notes that unplanned change and loss can present opportunities for inner freedom of a kind that has not been experienced before. Based upon your experiences, do you think this is true?

14. Spiritual ancestors emphasize the stripping away of one's ego-self as a prerequisite for experience of communion with the Ineffable. What might this stripping away of ego-self mean in your everyday life?

15. Saints and sages experienced the Ineffable as Infinite Love and an indwelling presence that holds all things in existence. What in your experience may affirm or question this? Is your answer connected to your perceptions of aging and loss?

16. Ancient masters emphatically stated that there is no separation between matter and spirit, life's circumstances and spirituality. What implications might this have for living in retirement and into old age?

Lightning Source UK Ltd.
Milton Keynes UK
UKOW04f1640270115

245228UK00002B/115/P